AXIS PARE

A PARENT'S GUIDE
TO EATING DISORDERS

A PARENT'S GUIDE TO

EATING DISORDERS

Tyndale House Publishers
Carol Stream, Illinois

Visit Tyndale online at tyndale.com.

Visit Axis online at axis.org.

Tyndale and Tyndale's quill logo are registered trademarks of Tyndale House Ministries.

A Parent's Guide to Eating Disorders

Copyright © 2023 by Axis. All rights reserved.

Cover illustration by Lindsey Bergsma. Copyright © Tyndale House Ministries. All rights reserved.

Designed by Lindsey Bergsma

Scripture quotations are taken from the Holy Bible, *New International Version,*® *NIV.*® Copyright © 1973, 1978, 1984, 2011 by Biblica, Inc.® Used by permission. All rights reserved worldwide.

For information about special discounts for bulk purchases, please contact Tyndale House Publishers at csresponse@tyndale.com, or call 1-855-277-9400.

Library of Congress Cataloging-in-Publication Data

A catalog record for this book is available from the Library of Congress.

ISBN 978-1-4964-6746-1

Printed in the United States of America

29	28	27	26	25	24	23
7	6	5	4	3	2	1

We turn skeletons into goddesses
and look to them as if they might
teach us how not to need.

MARYA HORNBACHER,
*WASTED: A MEMOIR OF ANOREXIA
AND BULIMIA*

CONTENTS

A LETTER FROM AXIS

Dear Reader,

We're Axis, and since 2007, we've been creating resources to help connect parents, teens, and Jesus in a disconnected world. We're a group of gospel-minded researchers, speakers, and content creators, and we're excited to bring you the best of what we've learned about making meaningful connections with the teens in your life.

This parent's guide is designed to help start a conversation. Our goal is to give you enough knowledge that you're able to ask your teen informed questions about their world. For each guide, we spend weeks reading, researching, and interviewing parents and teens in order to distill everything you need to know about the topic at hand. We encourage you to read the whole thing and then to use the questions we include to get the conversation going with your teen—and then to follow the conversation wherever it leads.

As Douglas Stone, Bruce Patton, and Sheila Heen point out in their book *Difficult Conversations*, "Changes in attitudes and behavior rarely come about because of arguments, facts, and attempts to persuade. How often do *you* change your values and beliefs—or whom you love or what you want in life—based on something someone tells you? And how likely are you to do so when the person who is trying to change you doesn't seem fully aware of the reasons you see things differently in the first place?"[1] For whatever reason, when we believe that others are trying to understand *our* point of view, our defenses usually go down, and we're more willing to listen to *their* point of view. The rising generation is no exception.

So we encourage you to ask questions, to listen, and then to share your heart with your teen. As we often say at Axis, discipleship happens where conversation happens.

Sincerely,
Your friends at Axis

---

[1] Douglas Stone, Bruce Patton, and Sheila Heen, *Difficult Conversations: How to Discuss What Matters Most*, rev. ed. (New York: Penguin Books, 2010), 137.

MENTAL HEALTH, PHYSICAL MANIFESTATIONS

BESIDES INCREASES in mental health issues such as anxiety and depression, today's teens also face increasing risks of developing eating disorders as a way to cope with their reality.[1] Because there are myriad websites and organizations dedicated to educating the public about eating disorders and to helping sufferers find lasting recovery, this guide will hopefully serve to educate you on how technology and culture contribute to the problem. In addition, we hope to provide a balanced Christian perspective on how to find true healing from a disease that affects both young and old, male and female, Christian and non-Christian alike. *(Note: we did our best not to link to sites that could be triggering for those struggling with eating disorders, except when necessary. If you choose to search for things mentioned in this guide, please do so at your own risk. It can be simultaneously horrifying and heartbreaking.)*

Disclaimer: *Information contained in this resource is intended only to increase knowledge and provide faith-based encouragement to users on the subjects of eating disorders, mental health, and other related issues. Axis does not intend to offer medical advice or treatment of any kind. The tools we offer are intended as tools only, the use and results of which should be confirmed by a qualified health-care professional. This information is not a replacement for diagnosis or treatment by a professional. Axis cannot be held responsible for actions taken without professional medical guidance.*

Besides increases in mental health issues such as anxiety and depression, today's teens also face increasing risks of developing eating disorders as a way to cope with their reality.

WHAT ARE THE BASICS I NEED TO KNOW?

HERE ARE SOME HELPFUL RESOURCES to consult as you begin to learn about this topic:

- **Eating disorders defined:** https:// www.mayoclinic.org/diseases -conditions/eating-disorders /symptoms-causes/syc-20353603

- **List of eating disorders (plus a list of less-common disorders):** https://www.nationaleating disorders.org/warning-signs-and -symptoms; https://en.wikipedia .org/wiki/Eating_disorder#Other

- **Who is most at risk:** https://www .anred.com/who.html

- **Causes and risk factors of eating disorders:** https://www.nami.org /About-Mental-Illness/Mental-Health -Conditions/Eating-Disorders

Many celebrities have struggled with eating disorders, which can serve to glamorize them in teens' eyes (especially because teens have a window into celebs' lives through social media). These celebrities include Zayn Malik (singer), Troian Bellisario (actress, *Pretty Little Liars*), Demi Lovato (singer and Disney star), Kesha (singer), Zoë Kravitz (actress, the Divergent series), Candace Cameron Bure (actress, *Full House*), and Shawn Johnson East (Olympic gymnast)—and if you don't know any of these names, you might remember this one: Karen Carpenter.

Many celebrities have struggled with eating disorders, which can serve to glamorize them in teens' eyes (especially because teens have a window into celebs' lives through social media).

WHAT ARE THE NOT-SO-BASICS I NEED TO KNOW?

SADLY, THERE'S AN ENTIRE SUBCULTURE on the Internet that encourages and promotes eating disorders.[2] Pro-anorexia (usually Pro-Ana) and pro-bulimia (Pro-Mia) websites abound, and a quick Google search will yield countless blogs and Tumblrs that detail weight-loss goals and methods, as well as tips for avoiding attention from concerned family and friends. One can also find "thinspiration" (or "thinspo," images that range from thin to downright skeletal) in less than a second via a search engine or by searching hashtags like #ana, #mia, #thinspo, #thighgap, #bonespo (bone inspiration), and #EDfam on any social network (though many are now closely monitoring and trying to censor this type of content).[3] However, specifically searching for these topics isn't the only way to find them; simply entering phrases like "fitness tips," "fitspiration/fitspo," or "weight loss" can also be an introduction to the world of eating disorders.

ANA AND MIA?

SHORT FOR "ANOREXIA" AND "BULIMIA," the Pro-Ana community has created these personas (as well as #Debbie for depression and #Sue for suicide) as ways to "encourage" individuals to push through whatever "setbacks" or "temptations" they may be experiencing in achieving their goals. There are even sites listing the "Ten Commandments" of Ana and messages written from Ana's voice, many of which are harsh and tell a person never to be satisfied with his/her body.[4]

WHY ARE EATING DISORDERS ON THE RISE?[5]

THERE ARE MANY CONTRIBUTING FACTORS, but we believe that underlying all of them is our modern concept of freedom. Elsa from *Frozen* describes it best: "No right, no wrong, no rules for me! I'm free!" If freedom is the ability to do what I want whenever I want with whomever I want as long as I'm not hurting anyone else, then saying how much or how little a person should weigh or eat is confining, restrictive, and repressive. Though this definition of freedom is fundamentally flawed (as G. K. Chesterton put it in his book *Orthodoxy*, "The more I considered Christianity, the more I found that while it had established a rule and order, the chief aim of that order was to give room for good things to run wild"[6]), it is nevertheless the reigning principle that children are being taught by ads, magazines, celebrities, books, friends, social media, movies, music, YouTube, and virtually every other medium.

"The more I considered
Christianity, the more I
found that while it had
established a rule and
order, the chief aim of that
order was to give room for
good things to run wild."

—G.K. CHESTERTON

WHY WOULD SOMEONE WANT THIS?

UNDERSTANDING THE APPEAL of eating disorders can be hard, but it's of paramount importance. To do so, first think about our culture. Women (and increasingly men) are surrounded by images of perfectly sculpted, gorgeous, flawless bodies (yes, bodies . . . they're often depicted without heads[7]). And these images are typically connected in one way or another to some level of happiness (how else would companies sell products?). So young, impressionable minds see such images and connect physical appearance, beauty, thinness, and perfection with happiness, popularity, self-worth, and success. But now, unlike generations before, young people have screens in their pockets that encourage them to focus on their appearance while incessantly delivering these images of "beauty," whether they're looking for them or not.

Second, family and peer relationships can play *major* roles in whether or not someone develops an eating disorder. One man was fat-shamed as a child by his mother (because she learned it from her own mother), as well as bullied by his peers for being "ugly" and fat, which contributed to his eating disorders and other destructive addictions.[8] One woman witnessed her mother's yo-yo dieting, fear of "fat," and hatred of her body, which the woman inevitably learned and put into practice in her early tween and teen years.[9] Then, because of the praise and attention she received for being so thin, her disorder spiraled out of control. We cannot underestimate the power of relationships in our lives. And in our increasingly digital world, mean-spirited comments are so easy to send and may seem insignificant to the sender, but can wreak havoc on the receiver.

[Survivors of eating disorders] often mention controlling their bodies as a way to cope with the intense emotional pain from trauma, saying they can't control anything else, but they can control food.

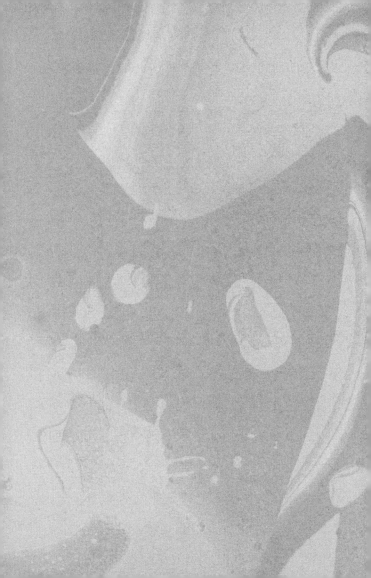

Third, many people with eating disorders don't view it as a problem to fix; rather, they see it as a lifestyle that's "worth it."[10] Many with eating disorders also mention that once they joined a pro-eating-disorder community online, they felt they finally had a place to belong. As one psychiatrist says, "Eating disorders can be extremely isolating conditions, and so finding a community of other people who think like you can be a powerful draw."[11] And because these communities are digital and often exclusive (i.e., hidden from concerned adults), the disorders become glamorized while the consequences of encouraging others to continue in their habits are never observed.

Finally, *many* survivors of eating disorders can pinpoint the beginning of their troubles to a traumatic experience: bullying/ridicule, abuse, a breakup, their parents' divorce, loss of a loved one, moving to a new place.[12] They often mention controlling their bodies as a way to cope with the intense emotional pain from that trauma, saying they can't control anything else, but they can control food. **Many turn to eating disorders not to get skinny, but to feel release from pain.**

WHAT ABOUT SPIRITUAL WARFARE?

WE KNOW THAT THE ENEMY "prowls around like a roaring lion looking for someone to devour."[13] He will use anything—an offhand comment, an advertisement, an insecurity, feeling left out or different, trauma, stress, peer pressure, loss of a loved one—to his advantage. His goal, as always, is to steal the abundant life Christ gives us. He does this by offering the very thing we long for: a sense of control, acceptance, community, to look a certain way, freedom from bullying . . .

Of course, whatever semblance of those things can be found through eating disorders and the pro-eating-disorder community is fleeting and incomplete, a sad and unsatisfying approximation of the true version of those desires, which is found only in Christ. But from the outside looking in, it's not easy to tell that this is the case, precisely because of the nature of counterfeits. Unless one is trained to notice the slight differences, to look beyond the immediate appearance, a counterfeit appears to be the real thing, but it leaves a person more empty, isolated, broken, and desperate than before.

When dealing with eating disorders, it's helpful to keep this in mind, both in how you pray and how you help someone who is suffering. But also remember that spiritual warfare may not be the direct cause of every eating disorder. The problem can also be linked to mental health issues, which can reinforce a skewed perspective of God, the world, and ourselves. We need to be mindful of both aspects, praying for protection against spiritual attack *and* for God to renew our children's minds.

[Eating disorders] can also be linked to mental health issues, which can reinforce a skewed perspective of God, the world, and ourselves.

IS THERE ANYTHING ELSE I SHOULD KNOW?

THERE ARE MANY WAYS for teens to keep in contact with their Pro-Ana friends. Even if you disable internet browsing on their devices, they can still use a friend's device to get online. One woman's concerned friend deleted her account on a Pro-Ana website, but the woman just got in touch with that community through an exercise app on her phone.[14] Unless your child wants to recover (more on that below), they will continue to find ways to connect with their pro–eating disorder friends, relating stories of "my crazy mom/dad/ friend who just doesn't get it and keeps trying to make me stop."

HOW CAN I TELL IF SOMEONE HAS AN EATING DISORDER?

SOME DISORDERS have physical manifestations (e.g., anorexia is marked by extreme weight loss and an obsession with calorie counting and exercise). Others aren't as obvious (anything that falls under OSFED, or "other specialized feeding or eating disorder"[15]), so take some time to familiarize yourself with the signs and symptoms of the different disorders, as well as to observe the person in question.[16] Monitoring online activities may also be revealing. The best way to really know is to ask your teen, but prayerfully and carefully consider this option. On the one hand, it may help them break the isolation, secrecy, and shame if you offer them a loving and safe environment in which to admit their struggles. On the other, they may not yet be ready to confront the issue or admit there's a problem, so asking about it could cause more harm than good.

WHAT DO I DO IF MY CHILD HAS AN EATING DISORDER?

ACTUALLY, DON'T DO ANYTHING . . . until you've had time to pray extensively, talk to experts and pastors, and formulate a strategy. As a mental illness, an eating disorder is an outward manifestation of a deeper problem.[17] That problem could involve bullying, sexual/physical/emotional abuse, an inability to cope with major life changes, pressure to look and act a certain way, unhealthy relationships, body dysmorphic disorder,[18] or something else entirely. Simply confronting the unhealthy relationship with food and exercise may, at best, miss the point altogether—or, at worst, compound the underlying issues, further pushing your teen into destructive behaviors. Anorexia has the highest mortality rate of any mental illness,[19] so taking the time to formulate a strategy and get your child the help they need can't be stressed enough.

Simply confronting the unhealthy relationship with food and exercise may, at best, miss the point altogether—or, at worst, compound the underlying issues, further pushing your teen into destructive behaviors.

PRAYER! Prayer is such a vital part of our lives, and it is the most important work we can do. Only God knows all the different facets of a person's struggles, and only He is powerful enough to deal with them and gracious enough to do so in the kindest way possible. So pray for your child and their heart often, but also pray *with* your child. Powerful things happen when we intercede for and on behalf of others. Though your child may not like it at first, they will come to see your heart and God's heart for them through the process.

Therapy. Depending on the extent and severity of the eating disorder, it may make sense to consider an inpatient treatment program in your area. If that's not the correct route for you, then we highly recommend finding a Christian therapist who specializes in eating disorder treatment. Because of the reality of spiritual

WHAT SHOULD I INCLUDE IN MY STRATEGY?

warfare, we believe that going through therapy that is not biblically based would ignore a very real and powerful component of your child's eating disorder. You may want to consider therapy for yourself as well. It would speak volumes to your child about how much you care if you're also willing to make changes.

A safe environment. A huge component of eating disorders is feeling different, unaccepted, and isolated. Make your home and your relationship with your child a safe place to talk through feelings, incidents, fears, insecurities, and relapses without fear of repercussions. **It's only in the light that we find freedom, not the darkness.**

Self-reflection. Though not always the case, teens often pick up unhealthy mentalities from their parents or another influential adult. If your home environment encourages disordered eating, that may be a big part of the problem. Take time to think about what was modeled to your child, and repent and ask God to forgive you for any unhealthy patterns. Repent to your child and ask them to forgive you as well. If your child observed disordered eating in someone else, open a discussion with your child about how this might have influenced them and whether it might be healing to talk to that person.

Restriction of privileges. This is an area that requires great wisdom and insight. But especially if you have a younger child, restricting their device and internet time may be necessary to keep harmful influences at bay. Some children just aren't mature enough to resist temptation or to make healthy choices on their own, so if possible, protect them. If you do go this route, always explain *why* you're setting certain boundaries—and keep the door open for discussion. Restrictions without explanations may be perceived as controlling and mean-spirited rather than loving and protective.

Patience. Sometimes the best thing we can do is get out of God's way and let Him do what He does best. You've said all you can say, you've offered every avenue of help you can, and now God needs time to move in your child's heart. God, in His omniscience, may be trying to teach you something as well. So make time to quiet yourself before the Lord and allow Him to speak to you. If we are intentional enough to be sensitive to His voice, He will reveal to us what we need to do and when we need to do it.

Only God knows all the different facets of a person's struggles, and only He is powerful enough to deal with them and gracious enough to do so in the kindest way possible.

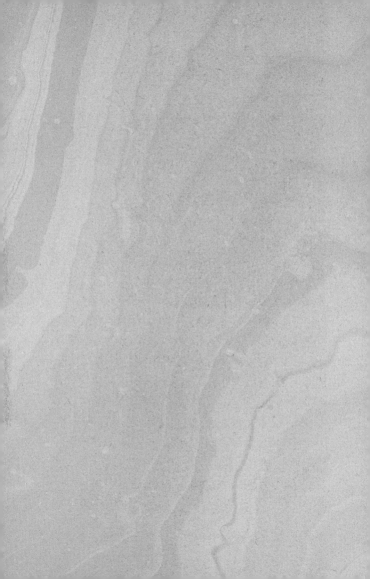

Scripture. If your child is willing, take time to search Scripture together for God's truth about our identity, worth, and value as children of God. Create a list of passages that you can pray together and over your child when they are struggling. If your child is not ready for this step, we still encourage you to do this for yourself so you can guide your prayers with Scripture. But *never* use the Bible to condemn your child. That will only compound their shame and feelings of not being good enough.

WHAT DO I DO IF MY CHILD DOESN'T WANT HELP OR WON'T ADMIT THERE'S A PROBLEM?

WATCHING SOMEONE willfully destroy their life is heartbreaking. If this is happening in your family, know that we understand your frustration, anger, sadness, and fear. But, as seen in relapsed drug addicts and alcoholics, until the motivation to change comes from within, people will continue to return to their destruction. Or, stated another way, until people understand they've settled for far less than the thriving, abundant life Christ offers, they will continue to believe there's no other way, that they've done the best they could with the hand they were dealt. No amount of nagging and pleading will solve the problem until the heart issues are confronted and rooted out.

Once you've lovingly communicated why you hope and pray for your child, the phrase "It's time to stop saying and start praying" may apply. Rather than beating

Any influence in your child's life, however small, is better than no influence.

your child over the head with stats, new treatment options, and rants about how they're destroying their life, rest in the assurance that your child knows where you stand. Then continue to pursue a relationship with them. **Any influence in your child's life, however small, is better than no influence.**

Note: You know your child and their circumstances best. In cases where serious physical harm or death may be imminent, intervention is needed. But in other cases, simply loving them, providing an open line of communication, and praying fervently may be much more effective than continuing to alienate by belaboring the point.

THE BOTTOM LINE

EATING DISORDERS aren't just terrible because of their physical effects; **they're horrible because they promise freedom and control, yet lead to total enslavement**— enslavement to image, comparison, others' opinions, secrecy, isolation, suffering, and never being enough. This is why eating disorders are so insidious, and it's what we need to focus on as we disciple others out of the grips of their eating disorders. "It is for *freedom* that Christ has set us free!"[20] That is, we were made for *true* freedom, the kind that is found within God's boundaries. Those boundaries keep evil out, allowing good to flourish. Jesus made the ultimate sacrifice so that we could "have life, and have it to the full."[21] We find that *only* through allowing God to control our lives, as scary as that might seem.

Those who suffer from eating disorders got to where they are because of one thing: fear. Fear of others' opinions, fear of abandonment, fear of ostracism, fear of what they felt inside, fear of heartache and suffering, fear of loss. Sometimes these fears have become so central to who they are, they can't bear to admit them, let alone let go of them.

God's Word is clear that fear has no place in our lives when we're filled with His love.[22] In fact, Jesus' number one imperative to us is to "fear not."[23] Why? Because the Lord knows that fear breeds insecurity, self-preservation, anger, dysfunction, and suffering, whereas love unlocks confidence, acceptance, self-sacrifice, peace, unity, flourishing, and grace. So, as Christ's ambassadors *and* as parents, it becomes our job to help those suffering from eating disorders embrace the love-filled abundant life—and no longer let their fears define them.

Eating disorders aren't just terrible because of their physical effects; they're horrible because they promise freedom and control, yet lead to total enslavement—enslavement to image, comparison, others' opinions, secrecy, isolation, suffering, and never being enough.

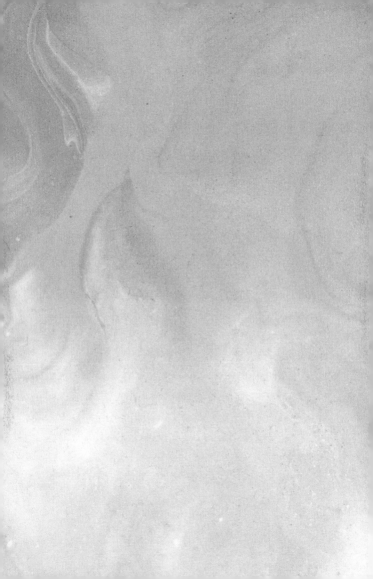

To do this, it's imperative that we see beyond the obvious physical manifestations to the deeper heart issues. It also means being willing to walk down the path of healing with our children. That may mean attending therapy with them, talking through past wounds, admitting fault where necessary, and not being too critical of them. When teens see that *real* freedom—the ability to be exactly who God made them to be—lies only in letting go of fear and control and turning it all over to God, they'll be ready to write a new story for themselves, one full of hope, redemption, mercy, and love.

God wants more than outward obedience. He wants to bring deep, lasting healing to your children's lives. Have patience and faith that He is already hard at work to make that happen!

In the meantime, may we devote ourselves to being part of God's plan of transformation by loving our children as Jesus loves us: by taking their burdens, by sacrificing our time and energy for them, by investing in them, by patiently drawing them out of their old selves and into their redeemed selves, and by driving out fear with love.[24]

RECAP

- Eating disorders have been glamorized in teens' eyes through media that promotes thinness and a perfect body as the way to happiness.

- Sadly, there are entire internet communities dedicated to encouraging and promoting eating disorders.

- Eating disorders are on the rise due to our modern definitions of freedom and happiness that are entirely determined by the individual.

- Some reasons teens develop eating disorders include our culture's unrealistic standards of beauty, a sense of community, and the desire to escape from internal pain.

- Eating disorders are a hard subject to broach, so it's important to pray, consult professionals, and form a strategy before taking any steps toward addressing the issue.

- If you're trying to help your child who has an eating disorder, therapy and a restriction of privileges are important, but providing a safe environment, giving them space for self-reflection, and demonstrating patience can be much more valuable.

- Your child may not be willing to address the problem right away. Nagging and pleading will not fix anything, but prayer and pursuing a relationship with your child will help them take the crucial step of personal motivation toward recovery.

If you're trying to help
your child who has an
eating disorder, therapy
and a restriction of
privileges are important,
but providing a safe
environment, giving them
space for self-reflection,
and demonstrating
patience can be much
more valuable.

DISCUSSION QUESTIONS

1. Have you ever known someone who struggled with an eating disorder? Did you talk with them about it?

2. Why do you think people develop eating disorders? Is it solely about how they look?

3. Do you know someone who has a good relationship with their body and with food? How did they get to that point?

4. How do you feel about your body? How do you feel about your life? Is there anything about your life or your body you wish you could change or that gives you anxiety? Why?

5. Why do you think people want control over their lives? Is it possible to have true control? What does God's Word say about living out of worry and fear?

6. How can I help you have a better relationship with yourself, your body, and others? Is there anything I've done that has affected those relationships negatively? How can I do better?

7. How can we pray for the people we know who struggle with eating disorders, mental health, and their identity? How else can we support them?

8. Do you feel safe enough to talk to me about your struggles, fears, and anxieties? If not, how can I help you feel safe?

ADDITIONAL RESOURCES

1. National Eating Disorders Hotline: (800) 931-2237

2. Eating Disorder Hope: https://www .eatingdisorderhope.com/recovery /faith-and-spirituality

3. "The Truth about Eating Disorders," Focus on the Family, https://www .focusonthefamily.com/parenting /the-truth-about-eating-disorders/

4. "Eating Disorders and the Power of Christ," The Gospel Coalition, thegospelcoalition.org/article/eating -disorders-and-the-power-of-christ/

5. "Eating Disorders," National Institute of Mental Health, https://www.nimh .nih.gov/health/topics/eating -disorders

6. "Eating Disorders," Nemours TeensHealth, https://kidshealth.org /en/teens/eat-disorder.html?WT.ac=

7. "Eating Disorder Treatment," National Eating Disorders, https://www.nationaleatingdisorders.org/treatment

NOTES

1. "What Are Eating Disorders?," National Eating Disorders Association, accessed June 1, 2022, https://www.nationaleatingdisorders.org/what-are-eating-disorders?inf_contact_key=c099af9b8c36f57bf78484db95cda1345a1d697ade63810d8cb3e9b7620706aa.

2. "Pro-Ana Websites: What You Need to Know," American Addiction Centers, updated November 11, 2021, https://americanaddictioncenters.org/anorexia-treatment/pro-ana.

3. Emily Reynolds, "Instagram's Pro-Anorexia Ban Made the Problem Worse," Wired, March 14, 2016, https://www.wired.co.uk/article/instagram-pro-anorexia-search-terms.

4. "Ana Lifestyle & Religion," Pro Ana Goddess, accessed June 1, 2022, https://proanagoddess.wordpress.com/ana-lifestyle-religion-2/; "A Letter from Ana," *Detroit Metro Times*, July 31, 2002, https://www.metrotimes.com/arts/a-letter-from-ana-2174214.

5. "What Are Eating Disorders?" National Eating Disorders Association.

6. G. K. Chesterton, *Orthodoxy* (Moscow, Idaho: Canon Press, 2020), 101.

7. "Killing Us Softly 4 - Trailer [Featuring Jean Kilbourne]," ChallengingMedia, YouTube, video, 4:56, August 24, 2012, https://www.youtube.com/watch?v=jWKXit_3rpQ&t=164s.

8. Raylene Hungate, "What Is Body Dysmorphia: Symptoms, Causes, and Treatment," Eating Disorder Hope, updated August 16, 2021, https://www.eatingdisorderhope.com/information/body-image/body-dysmorphia.

9. "Eating Disorder Awareness & Education," Eating Disorder Hope, updated May 11, 2017, https://www.eatingdisorderhope.com/information.

10. Sarah Emily Baum, "'Pro-Ana' Blogs Continue despite New Online Policies,'" Women's eNews, April 24, 2017, https://womensenews.org/2017/04/pro-ana-blogs-continue-despite-new-online-policies/; Sarah Rainey, "Secretly Starving," *Telegraph*, accessed June 1, 2022, http://s.telegraph.co.uk/graphics/projects/inside-the-world-of-anorexia-blogging/.

11. Rainey, "Secretly Starving."

12. "Stories of Hope," Eating Disorder Hope, accessed June 1, 2022, https://www.eating disorderhope.com/blog/category/stories -of-hope.

13. 1 Peter 5:8

14. Rainey, "Secretly Starving."

15. "Other Specified Feeding or Eating Disorder," National Eating Disorders Association, accessed June 1, 2022, https://www.national eatingdisorders.org/learn/by-eating-disorder /osfed.

16. Veronique Hoebeke, "7 Signs Your Friend or Family Member Is at Risk for an Eating Disorder," Resources to Recover, November 1, 2016, https://www.rtor.org/2016/11/01/signs -of-an-eating-disorder/?gclid=CNfU2b6z5tQC Fc22wAodU5UPPg; "Help & Support," National Eating Disorders Association, accessed June 1, 2022, https://www.nationaleatingdisorders .org/help-support.

17. "Eating Disorders," National Alliance on Mental Illness, accessed June 1, 2022, https:// www.nami.org/About-Mental-Illness/Mental -Health-Conditions/Eating-Disorders.

18. "Understanding Body Dysmorphic Disorder (BDD)," Anxiety & Depression Association of America, accessed June 1, 2022, https://adaa .org/understanding-anxiety/body-dysmorphic -disorder.

19. Gail Hamilton et al., "Anorexia Nervosa— Highest Mortality Rate of Any Mental Disorder: Why?," Eating Disorder Hope, updated February 8, 2018, https://www.eatingdisorderhope .com/information/anorexia/anorexia-death-rate.

20. Galatians 5:1, emphasis added.

21. John 10:10.

22. Debbie McDaniel, "33 Verses about Fear and Anxiety to Remind Us God Is in Control," Crosswalk, March 16, 2020, https://www .crosswalk.com/blogs/debbie-mcdaniel/33 -verses-to-remind-us--we-do-not-have-to -fear.html.

23. Rick McDaniel, "Faith over Fear: The Bible's #1 Statement Is 'Don't Be Afraid,'" *Christian Post*, November 5, 2014, https://www.christianpost .com/news/faith-over-fear-the-bibles-1 -statement-is-dont-be-afraid-129050/.

24. See 1 John 4:18.

PARENT GUIDES TO SOCIAL MEDIA
BY AXIS

It's common to feel lost in your teen's world. Let these be your go-to guides on social media, how it affects your teen, and how to begin an ongoing conversation about faith that matters.

BUNDLE THESE 5 BOOKS AND SAVE

PARENT GUIDES TO SOCIAL MEDIA

5 CONVERSATION STRATEGIES WITH YOUR TEEN

DISCOVER MORE PARENT GUIDES, VIDEOS, AND AUDIOS AT AXIS.ORG

axis

www.axis.org

CP1605